DOLLY MIXTURE

Dolly Mixture

Michela Volante

Dolly Mixture
Michela Volante

Published by Greyhound Self-Publishing 2021
Malvern, Worcestershire, United Kingdom.

Printed and bound by Aspect Design
89 Newtown Road, Malvern, Worcs. WR14 1PD
United Kingdom
Tel: 01684 561567
E-mail: allan@aspect-design.net
Website: www.aspect-design.net

Cover Design Copyright © 2021 Aspect Design
ISBN 978-1-909219-85-4

Dedicated to D

CONTENTS

Forgive me, brother

Not a sound to break the silence,
The hideous uncanny silence
Tall reeds worried by a restless breeze
Extend as far as eye can see
Never were the moors so bleak, never such a silence

From nowhere a significant drumming
– Forecast of impending storm?
Wilderbeest or zebra crossing open veldt?
No, for this is merrie England!
The drumming becomes a coarser rumbling

Out of the gloom appear the horsemen
Helmets and hilts reflect a tired sun
The day a weary one for Cromwell's men
Many loyalists have paid the price
Many heads have rolled upon the marsh

Rough snorts of steaming mares
Waft across the desolate fen
The captain halts 'neath a stately elm
Horses and riders claim brief respite
Helmets are strewn as curses fill the air

A diligent soldier inspects his bloody sabre
How many brothers has he slain this day?
How many 'filthy English' in these fair hills?
O deep sorrow and futility of this war
Never proud conquest, never gallant victory

No return from courageous French defeat
No acclaim amongst Elizabeth's ranks
Cheered by a worthy clamorous mob
Only a plundered cottage to lay ones head
A plundered English cottage

Yet he has his orders to kill his brethren
The ale gives courage, the money does more
He must root out the blaggards alien to the Cause
Frilled blaggards who yesterday fought at his side
Whose sole crime was to wish for a king

The sharp order rasps across the moor
As sun is setting men are mounting
Dust flies high as the column passes
Raucous laughter echoes a false musket shot
Slaughter, rape and pillage beckon the hurtling troupe

The thunder of hooves dies to a dull grumble
Dust settles as shapes are swallowed by the murk
The sun slides from view, the land dons its mystic cloak
Leaving the agonising ceaseless breeze
Never were the moors so bleak, never such a silence

❧

Prisons of Glass

Sealed within glass compartments
Strap-hanging and jostled together
Though never touching
Like test-tubes in a rack
Hung-up till the end of the line

Stealing furtive glances
Yet avoiding eye-contact
Waxwork figures, polyester uncrushed
Opaque faces, preserved in makeup, suntan, hormones
Differences smoothed out to a uniform orange

Sanitized with deodorant, aftershave
Air-brushed to perfection
Cosmopolitan airport dolls
Weaving towards Heath Row
Still heads, eyes turning from side to side
Each possessing the battery of ego and desire
The motivator, the chip that makes them human

A stranger among these glazed earthlings
I am trapped in their future vacuum
Allowed to glimpse their alien culture
Suspended in their gleaming capsule
Awaiting my rude ejection into the past

❧

Dark House

The suffering, the pain
Had all been in vain
The bell in its frame
Would not ring again
Above the dark house

No sparrows flutter
From belfry to eave
The web on your sleeve
Warns you to leave
The dark house

High over your head
The bats on the rafter
Know what you came after
You left all your laughter
Outside the dark house

Beneath rotting porch
Your servant stands tall
– Til you enter the hall
And then starts to crawl
Like a church mouse

He shows you his claw
As he closes the door
And the cage you ignore
Has straw on the floor
The music is Strauss

The lock it snaps tight
You count all your scars
As through rusty bars
You gaze up at the stars
Your home – the dark house

Over shoulder you spy
The demons again
Come in from the rain
To recline in your brain
The setting is Faust

Through swirling mist
Your temptress is there
With snakes in her hair
Her desires laid bare
As a slab of cold stone

The trial was a fix
They are in the end
Yes, you're condemned
Eternity to spend
Within the dark house

Your executioner draws nigh
The light it fades fast
Black holocaust
You surrender at last
To the dark house

❧

Sonnet
(with apologies to a certain Warwickshire bard)

Shall I compare thee to a winter's hoare?
Thou art more cold and more hard of heart
Trees overhang the barren earth with icy tentacles
And season's hold doth dull the brightness of your eyes

The sheen and lustre of those golden tresses
Turneth, it seems, to leaden grey
The sunlight that gave that olive glow
Fades as transient summer wanes too soon

And I can no longer love you to the end
The coldness of winter's gloom proclaims
Eternity to be too long a time
And I must, in sadness, seek my solace
And lay my head upon a warmer place

❧

Priceless Pearl

Happiness, it comes and goes
Along some cobbled street
Within a crowded market-place
Where old friends chance to meet

Sometimes the price is high
Wherever a heart is bought,
But how soon it dissolves
Whenever love is fraught

The pearl is lost to those
Who, sullied from their birth
Are doomed to search in vain
Vast corners of the earth

Thence to recall in memory
On days lived out alone
Where fleeting genial glimpses
Mocked they'd found a home

Retrieving this treasured pearl
Eludes the mind of man
How often is it grasped
Within a brief life-span?

❧

It's All in the Game

When it's a question of sport
I'm not found in field, pitch or court
Though to many I know it's appealing
I'd rather be weeding
Or even force-feeding
Or counting the flies on the ceiling

Now, I'm not crazy for golf
Never waited on Palmer's putt
Not for the eye of the Tiger I hanker
Nor wander the long grass
In the wake of Jack Niclaus
From birdie and eagle to bunker

Now if there's foul play
Along the fairway
I say this without word of malice
I'm not missing a thing
Without Faldo's swing
Nor living next-door to Alliss

With cricket is there a point?
To me KP is just nuts
Maybe Marcus' off-drive is a pleasure
When Monty turns in a haul
My eye's just not on the ball
Though of Yousuf he's got the measure

Remember when pavilions rang
With muted handclaps from the boundary
At Edgbaston, the Oval or Lords?
The majesty of gentle off-breaks?
Now they don't have what it takes
It's silly costumes, hooters and hordes

Never been bowled over by billiards
Nor snared by snooker's success
– Missed my cue again
Though Parrot and Davis are gents
The boredom I feel is intense
The colours give me a migraine

Hard to keep score
On a black and white screen
Mountjoy and Rearden supreme,
Nobody could knock it
'Pot Black' was the name of the frame
But what fuss when it fell in the pocket

Heavens above, 'Two sets to Love'!
(Since Edberg and Borg centre court is a morgue
– Better have never been seen}
For me it's an excuse
To practice verbal abuse
And eat copious strawberries and cream

Pavlova, Corsitzoff and Dropawitch
The players are all new
Speed agility and curses abound
Yes, it's faster today
We've got Andy they say
We'll be cheering from Murray-mound

Football comes under the hammer
And I'm not into blood sports
This one has attracted the mockers
Such hype and aggression
Such tackle for possession
In a word could only be soccer's

They've all the stars, from Lampard to Coles
One small problem – the scoring of goals
Then there're the wives, the cash and the booze
The waywardness, debauchery and sex
From Adams to Best, from Rooney to Becs
Is it a wonder they always Loos?

Who wins or who yields
The cups or the shields
Whatever the outcome, whatever befalls
Kick them or bowl them
Lob, screw or hole them
To me it's a load of old balls!

℘

Dark Corridors of Mind

Empty silence so unkind
Words falling out of place
A corridor of mind
Upon the mirror of a face

The puzzle on the table
Pieces scattered on the floor
Foretell a simple fable
Vacant eyes upon a door

A book that's left unread
The slightest chill of fear
Fermenting in a head
Like a bottle of sad beer

A cup of flawed blue chips
The tearful silent prayer
Drawn from thin cracked lips
That whisper of despair

The snapshot on the wall
Recalls an image well defined
Of a voice in a lonely hall
Along a corridor of mind

❧

The G-force of Love
(ode to a lost glove)

We were always together
Sharing hotdogs or mulled wine in plastic cups
Holding sparklers, ski-poles or tiny pups
How could you go? How could you leave?
Not even a bye your sleeve

Don't those moments mean a thing to you?
Though smitten with each-other
We weren't a'mitten to each-other
We've always been so hand in love
You being there was just enough

Lying side by side cuddled in a bag
Happiness was in our grasp
They said we made a handsome pair, my other half
Will I find another partner? not one like you
I'm so lost, no you're so lost!
How shall I cope with permafrost?

We clasped each-other in the rain
Built a snowman and christened it
We were so alike, such a perfect fit
Spick and span we hung out together
In all weathers on the line
Those who said you were into leather
Pulled the wool over your eyes and mine

I should have seen it all along
You were a dab-hand at deception
There was that time in reception
When you wandered off alone
I found you hiding behind the phone

Can't we hold it together?
Keep in touch, you're in demand
You always lent a helping hand
We said side by side we'd settle
Hold a brolly, grasp a nettle

I admired your hands-on approach
You were into everything
Always there in the coldest snaps
Sharing our applauding claps
You and me driving cars
You and me on handlebars

Tucked up tight in our compartment
Not knowing what 'to part' meant
We would grab every unmissed chance
To meet in pockets of resistance
Our fingers used to intermingle
It's just no fun now being single

Yet, on the other hand...
Leaving like that I feel entrapped
You really want your knuckles rapped
Now I'll end up being scrapped
Or worse left on the shelf
To be recycled as a Christmas elf

Or maybe, just maybe, we'll meet again
You'll appear beside the road
And we'll forget this episode,
Or wave at me from fence or hedge
And we'll renew our tender pledge
Then we'll end this poignant pause
And join together in warm applause

℘

Call in on Mr Chung
(or Bull in a China Shop)

Stomp snow from your boots in the hall
As the mercury sinks to its lowest ebb
Pass the barometer that hangs on the wall
Claiming fine and sunny within its web

Black alligator grins from the windowsill
Sleek scaled sliver twinkling by candlelight
And winks at proud pelican with sagging bill
Beyond the casement moon scans eerie night

The little rainbow man from Peking
Relaxing on his ivory cushions
Holds us spellbound when he's speaking
His walls papered with escutcheons

Flowerpots high on oaken settles
The long mural of the queen of Orange
Hangs above neat rows of copper kettles
And purple daffodils he'd rearrange

In a corner stands the black telephone
That takes him into the fifth dimension
Against the spinning wheel the saxophone
Will be played with the best intention

The notes issued may sound peculiar
From the floor or any position
As grandfather ticks they grow groovier
Heard in the attic by the silver physician

After a game of chequers or mah-jong
His deep brow furrowed and face a mask
With knowing smile he will hum a song
While taking tea from a poppy cask

From the eaves coos the embroidered albatross
Then lands on his shoulder in a piece of eight
Drooping moustache twitches like fine floss
As he tells of what we should appreciate

Pineapple cups and a paper jelly
Adorn a table of elegant style
Matching the dragon across his belly
The ceiling enhanced in cherry-stone tile

Above his head amid ornamental filigree
Glint gaily colored rows of wine bottles
Gold and green and deep red they sway
Over a chinese vase of insipid mottles

Beneath the shiny sounding gong
The evil cat-grin of the Siamese
Stares through you the room along
Until you crawl upon your knees

From this haze of eastern magic
In his many-colored suit of silk
He tells tales, some gay some tragic
Of pagodas, lanterns, goats without milk

Of rickshaws and seventeen chop-sticks
Brass bamboo and lotus-blossom twigs
Coca-cola and china tea do not mix
And men wear the powder and the wigs

თ

Sardines

Every morning
The hustle the bustle
The turmoil again
Every evening
Into the melee
The rush for the train

Here's Smith and Wilson
Heading for Edgeware Road
There's Ms Bambridge
With that pimply toad

Zip – the doors open
Pile 'em inside
Squeeze 'em up tight
Enjoy the ride

Often a pickpocket
Never a cop
Pushing and shoving
Off at next stop

Sweating room only
A glower and a cuss
On the Victoria Line
To Oxford Circus

The struggle to get there
By any means
Buffeted, dishevelled
Playing sardines

☙

Between the Eyes

Eyes that peep, eyes that despise
Eyes that weep or sympathise
Eyes that beseech, eyes that glow
Eyes that bewitch, eyes for show

Eyes for rejection
Eyes for deception
Eyes for recollection
Eyes for introspection

Eyes for reaction
Eyes for attraction
Eyes for distraction
Eyes for transaction

Hard eyes that glare
Moist eyes that care
Dark eyes that snare
Blank eyes that stare

Eyes of multi-coloured hue
Depending upon point of view
Eyes of many shades of blue
Eyes of amber, hazel too

Eyes of silver or eyes of green
And all colours in between
Hard to chose between the eyes
Her's the colour of autumn skies

⌀

The Fairies

'Tis de fairies,' they said
When they lost their pet monkey
'Fairies, dey took 'im,
Like O'Flaugherty's donkey'

When Josh Tanner broke a leg
After too many down at the Bush
'It's de fairies,' he claimed
'Dey gave me a push.'

When Mic the butcher found that gold coin
Fairies again took the blame
When Mollie's horse came first at the show
The cry that went up was the same

Dentist Phil McCavity won 50 pund
And it was obvious who was at fault
Named and shamed, cussed and blamed
Somehow they never got caught

When squire's wife gave birth to twins
And tears turned her eyes ruby red
'Squire's bin away, in England two years
– Away with de fairies!' they said.

⁊

winter solace

can I ever catch you
– on bramble-snagging moor
running through the tangled fern
where blackbirds give mournful song
and peat fires gently burn?

could this be you
– a rustling in the trees
– the lantern at my door
– cascades of watery sunlight
that caress the forest floor?

you gently sigh,
last night's gales were long
and filled your heart with awe
but since the curse was lifted
your laughter rings once more

from a high plateau
my lazy blue eyes
gaze on winter's empty face
yet I recall fleeting moments
when I shared your space

once, in the pulsing dusk
beneath frosty star-sparkle
a minstrel left his mountain
whisked you through purple twilight
to the hidden mystic fountain

within my dreams,
numbered as chandeliered raindrops
framing silver opalescent hillsides;
in the calm beyond the storm
the reverie abides

❧

Martyr Martha

Martha was a puritan
Who hallowed all the Saints
In between she spent her time
With her canvas and her paints

Her husband was a tartar
A man made for the rules
Dull and very drab was he
But learn-ed in the schools

'Martha, paint my portrait,
Hang it high upon yon' wall':
I hear they painted Cromwell
With 'is warts an' all!'

'He may be Lord Protector
But he's same as common folk'
She said it with conviction
But meant it as a joke

'Common as you and me:
and what you may think funny,
They didn't do it for 'is looks
They did it for 'is money!'

&

Vista

She had stared from her casement forever
Through the rain of many tears
He never came

Through the icy blizzard of long winters
She clung frozen to the windowsill
He never came

Icicles pierced her warm heart
Until her salty tears froze over
Still he did not find her

Searching steamy piazzas in heat-heavy noons
And waited longingly at cappuccino tables
He never came

Suddenly when she had turned to stone
At last he appeared before her
With eyes of solitude
She stared blankly back

Patiently he coaxed warmth
To melt her gaze of glass
He brought her colour
He brought her light

Now she stares from her window
In sadness that he came so late
His hands hold hers
Gently he kisses her eyelids
She blinks and he is gone

Yet peering cautiously
Her soulful eyes glimpse
The faintest rainbow beyond the storm
Imperceptibly
She begins to smile

❧

Dickhead the Third
(the bard strikes again)

Now is the summer of our indolence
Made mawkish winter by this rain of Huddersfield
And all the sunspots that cause us to wear Rayban UV8s
Are lost to a Force Nine from Barnsley
Now are our knuckle-dusters and chains
Hung up as ornaments in Ma's living room
Grim Job Centres have been freshly painted and upgraded
Now, instead of mounting barded Nortons
To race up the A1 and frighten old codgers on mopeds
I am forced to caper nimbly in my lady's chamber
To the muted strains of Miles Davis
But being shaped for sportish tricks
I catcheth my reflection in the basement window
As I stomp the snow away outside No 43
The home of some wanton ambling nymph

Yet I who art so nobly formed
Fair of feature and Adonis-like in my stride
Blessed and beautified by assembling nature
Trendy, replete in no compromise black leather and Martins
Bedecked in a make-over by Revlon
That dogs do fawn at my feet
Espying my silhouette in the sun
Am reminded of Brad Pitt, Mel Gibson and Leo DeCaprio
Rolled into one
I who am too perfectly proportioned, and hung
To soil my Docs on dusty highways

I who am such a mega-stud
Do tireth greatly of the scene in the Old Kent Road
And the idle pleasures of the millenium dome

I'm a reformed character, I've served out my Asbo
To whit I'm preserving precious time
To taketh garments to Oxfam
To write to Amnesty International
And to return abandoned supermarket trolleys
Plots and schemes I've hatched, seemingly innocent in
    conception
By libels, prophecies and copious quantities of 6% German
    lager
To set my brother Clint and his probation officer
In rapturous love the one with the other
And, as I am so warm and kind-hearted a person
This day shall Clint be set verily tamping
When he learns he hath a good record and his slate is
    washèd clean.
Dive thoughts, down to my boots: here Clint cometh.

೧

Humpy Dumpy
(HD – high flyer or heavy liar?)
Financial Crisis 2008

Humpy Dumpy sat in Wall Street
But the Stock market took a major defeat
All the politicians and all the wise men
Couldn't put the market together again

'The future's bleak, the country's disowned us!
What do we care, we'll still get our bonus!
We only wanted a brief little flutter –
Not our money, we'll not end in the gutter!'

Now the question I ask you investors
You savers, hoarders and egg-nesters
Was HD a bountiful benevolent banker
Or just a worthless waster and ......?

☙

*(Humpty Dumpty sat on a wall
Humpty Dumpty had a great fall
All the kings horses and all the kings men
Couldn't put Humpty together again)*

Them There Eyes!

The eyes have it, the eyes have it!
Look closer, what is there?
Read the laughter, read the curious
Go further if you dare

The radio plays Billie Jean
Cuban boas catch bats in caves
Lights flash red, amber, green
Much upon these eyes engraved

Thru' mist these eyes have seen
Serenaded by tambourine
The hobo and the squeaky clean
Both submerged in a submarine

She ran out when the cash ran out
To keep the faith she was unable
Our warm wanderings stood for nowt
Soon she left my breakfast table

Those eyes seldom shared my vision
Sometimes careless with the truth
We shared bitter sweet reflections
And a taste for gin and vermouth

Love the beautiful sexy eyes
Chestnut and sultry they tantalise
But what of when the laughter dies
Behind them, there the sadness lies

☙

Hostage

No more I'll pay ransom to those dark eyes
Made my homage, served my time
Sacrificed at the holy shrine

No more shall her beautific shade beguile
Binding shackles cast aside
Fling those darkened shutters wide

No more imprisoned in sweet love's embrace
Unfettered I pen this rhyme
Reverie shall now be mine

Away with that desperate haunting vestige
Though she'll reach me as before
As the sea returns to shore

Reconciled to not forget, yet not mourn
But blessing each devout dawn
Sentient though not forlorn

☙

December's Cruel Legacy

Chase the crisp dead leaves
That skip away
Hither and wither
As fleeting memories

Wizened brown husks
Dark veins standing proud
Like lurid life lines
Cast adrift – ended though unended

Twisted, torn and tattered
Frayed and scattered
Crushed and broken
(too brief those spells of sunlight)
They rake the barren 'scape

Fickle as unwritten unnumbered pages
Abandoned to the winds of change
They dance across those bitter stages
To the tune of winter's rages
They taunt and tease the sterile plane
Yet fail to stir the pen

❧

Mr Chung Revisited

Solid oak creaks to lovely Tiger Lee
Glide along a laughing-mirror hall
Cheongsam rustles as she follows slowly
Through a mist of pink incense over all

Beneath the bell-tower of the flying bat
She pauses before a door of harlequin
Signals you to enter with the purr of a cat
As the sound of the gong heralds you in

Adjust your eyes to the beat of the humming-bird
Scarlet chinese lantern casts shadows on the wall
There sits Mr Chung as if he had not heard
You enter, around his shoulders a purple shawl

Sipping green tea from a cup of quicksilver
He strokes the cat with the terrible eyes
At a breeze from the lattice the wick will stir
On the candle that twinkles up to the skies

With grace he displays Ming Dynasty coins
And paintings of bamboo houses and scrolls
Summons Tiger Lee where the partition joins
The fleur-de-lys wall, as the grand gong tolls

Spreading willow is spied from your couch
Through the geraniums on the window-sill
Catch the aroma from the tobacco pouch
As he rolls choice leaf clay pipe to fill

Golden eagle watches from his lofty perch
As a chilly zephyr trembles a rubber plant
Across the lawn by stately silver-birch
Soft paper roses are pruned by the sergeant

High on the wall hangs the buffalo carcass
With unseeing eyes he surveys the masquerade
Mr Chung smiles and takes snuff from a vase
As light from the candle begins to fade

Tiger Lee enters with oriental dishes
Suey, bean sprouts and soy sauce in bowls
Oysters and rolls fulfil our wishes
With cool Chablis to warm our souls

Downing chopsticks we turn to the fruit
Pineapples pomegranates, lemon bananas
Upon the table by the silver flute
And Wedgwood jar that holds sultanas

With cider lips nibble a macaroon
Sip tea from a cup of floral décor
Stir with a rusty runcible spoon
Do not spill on leopard-skin floor

Take your leave of this mystical man
Leave the kaleidoscope to return again
Through the maze that forms a life-span
Of orchid flowers and parasols in the rain

ဆ

Impeachment of the Heart

'Mad about you...'
– 'Lost without you...'
– 'Happy ever after...'
Empty phrases discovered in some musty drawer

Dead Sea phrases
Washed-up on a tide of dreams
Beached and bleached from seasons of neglect
A flotsam of feelings scattered along shores of sunder

Forgotten fragments
Fashioned in the heat of passion
Fired in the kilns of complacency
Lying distorted and ambiguous

Precious legacies located in dark corners,
Filtered through the prism of time and decay,
Trigger tormenting images
In the museum of the mind

Cautiously we pick up the pieces
Of fleeting faces, light and shade
And patiently sift the evidence
For the impeachment of the heart

℅

Alla Tristezza

Upon the broken violin of you and I
I'll pluck but one more note.
An unfinished symphony of jaded sequences
And reflections on a soulful interlude
Prelude to a dying swan of poignant hope
And still-born dreams of bliss.
Our majestic overtures subsumed
By the swelling tempo of life.

⁓

Putney Bridge

Above, the vault is a translucent blue
Beneath, rippling current holds a greyish hue
Turbans and saris approach the water's edge
A speedboat rocks at anchor below the ledge

Sample an Aloo Gosht at a restaurant you pass
With Chapati, Papadum or Jalebi Madras
Dust stings my eyes as I climb the ridge
No, this is not India but Putney Bridge

Pass the stone parapet of All Saints towers
And miniature gardens decorated with flowers
To London city after three or four mile
My feet are cemented, here I'll linger awhile

Telephone and police box below ICT
Joining Putney with Fulham, north to Chelsea
To port lies Richmond, serene and in splendour
Away to the starboard the Westminster agenda

A pleasant pleasure steamer tacks by beneath
Above, red giants pass on to Putney Heath
Eyes survey the scene, from a 255, 30 or 22
For Clapham Junction, Kingston, London Zoo

People cross the river, backwards and forth
From north to south and from south to north
By foot, and machines of all colours and sorts
From trucks and hondas to saloons and sports

Harassed mother and child, ladies in fur coats
Old men leaving their mind upon the boats
Lad with cheese-roll, one day I'll be a man,
Pulls faces at tired pregnant woman with pram

Nightly lit by trident clusters of sulphur glow
And reds and greens that demand stop then go
Gaily lit hotels kaleidoscope the river mist
Till dawn breaks and the bridge is sun-kissed

Misty young beauties, golden legs and smiles
Hurry to station past blocks with deep-red tiles
Small girl holds hands with an austere aunt
Couples watch anglers at their favourite haunt

Call in for a pint at the Eight Bells sign
On the northern bank by the District Line
Where the beer is good, a lunch-hour to pass,
Folks are friendly and sometimes there's jazz

Shops hum with the chase for a bargain
Silk scarf and apples then back on the train
Turning wheels and time are racing away
For a brief moment on the bridge I will stay

❧

Study in Umbra

Pitch black was the night
And late the hour
No moon's blessed light
Above the dark tower

No merry laughter
No gay spinning dancers
Evil bats on the rafter
Over drab necromancers

Maniacs cavort across the floor
Pursuing the occult
Behind the stout studded door
Secured by a rusty bolt

Demons summoned from afar
Corroding insanity's vice
Drinking blood from a musty jar
Amid the flames of sacrifice

Satanists rule the night
Reciting a dreadful rhyme
In sickening appetite
The naked bodies entwine

Black candles, poison charms
The image of the Goat
Seeking malicious harm
With sacrilegious note

The leader writhes in fright
Trapped within his curse
No escape, the bolt holds tight ·
No fiend can disperse

As the smoke climbs higher
The one they've called has come
All are consumed by fire
The world is purged, but numb

❧

Fata Morgana

(A sort of mirage occasionally seen in the Straits of Messina.
'Fata' is Italian for 'fairy' and the fairy Morgana was the sister of
Arthur and pupil of Merlin. She lived at the bottom of a lake,
and dispensed her treasures to whom she liked.)

No more shall those sweet lips beguile
No more I'll jig to that distant drum
No more enraptured by that smile
For now I bow to a different sun

Not bewitched by dark eye sparkle
No more to feel that warm embrace
No more dazzled by that dimple
Spreading the smile across her face

No more shall her warm touch tingle
As she places her hand in mine
No cool fingers intermingle
No more the subtle scent Sabine

No more her silken tones invite
As haunting thoughts return anew
She always knew my lies were white
And also knew my love was true

Randomly she'll return I know
I'll not allow complete surrender
She'll not ensnare me, this I vow
Yet waning fire retains an ember

So time has called an end to grief
Although the spectre stays alive
And time may bring blessed relief
Although a trace of her survives

Camogli

Do bells chime o'er Figari's climb
Is Cristina preparing the sheets
Does the owl still own the night
And traffic screech in the streets

Is the sun pouring over Camogli
As boats pull away on the tides
While churches toll out the Sabbath
And Garibaldi's ghost still glides

Is the pullman to Genoa on track
As the palms sway in the breeze
Is the senora issuing tickets
Efficient and eager to please

Does a train pause at Margherita
Then pass on to Sestri Levante
Do the sun-lovers rule the beaches
In sun-kissed bikinis so scanty

Does the blithe monk grace Frutuosso
Where Christ rises 'neath the waves
In the bay where tourists are swimming
Surf-boarding, exploring the caves

Is the boat still moored at the jetty
With bronzed salts awaiting the tide
Is there time for seafood spaghetti
Before Portofino is spied

Do walkers still climb to San Rocco
In the glare of the noonday sun
Do they pause at the bar of Pippi
As many before them have done

Does Rosetta serve at the trattoria
Where rowdy Americans gather
Is the boss as slick (runs a tight ship)
With cronies and wine-time blather

Do the boats call at Camogli
On the way to Genoa port
Does the swaying Med sparkle
Where debacle or battle was fought

Sharing a strong sense of direction
All join in the merry rumpus
In the wake of senore Columbus
They do it without a compass

ℰℑ

Old Wyves-Tale

'Where were you, my busty fakir
My bed-nag – my porridge baker?'
'My dear, you looked so poorly
Lying there in all your glory,
That I went across four-acre
Saw T. Jones the undertaker.'

'Woman, you presume too much
Your evil-eye and bramble touch!
What do you keep me living for?
You've driven me outside death's door
With your mousy hair and wrinkled skin
I think it's worse outside than in!'

'Here's your soap and shaving water–'
He said something he didn't oughta
The old house collapsed and caught her
Buried alive in bricks and mortar
Her husband of course was used to her
You see his name it was St Lucifer

❧

Positive Negative

What is love anyway – an idea?
(Freud thought it an illusion)
Does it transform the ordinary?
Stealthily it absorbs us
As, immersed in chemicals,
A vision feints in upon the page
Gently at first,
Slowly deepening and strengthening
Until it's finally, indelibly there

The dark room of love in the mind
– At first, when she looked at me
It meant really nothing...
Gradually, imperceptibly
Her image stole over the blank sheet
Of my searching soul
Until it took possession of me
Now she's all over me
Never to be erased

&

Forked Tongues

My hope lies in language
Adrift in a bullrush basket
Lined with flags and reeds
Caulked in tar and clay

'Confuse their tongues!'
I meander babbling waters
Tossed, rejected, misunderstood
I drift erratically

Seeking a kindred spirit
I am hurled far and wide
To enter uncharted icy currents
That sear me to the bone

Thence to float sun-baked
Crusted and berry-brown
Blind to the force that drives me
To the arms of Pharoh's daughter

❧

In My Fashion
(Hamlet Act III Sc I –
Shakespeare did have a sense of humour, didn't he?)

To lie or not to lie, that is the question.
Whether 'tis nobler in the mind to suffer
The slings and arrows of outrageous honesty
Or take up arms against a sea of unpalatable axioms
And by opposing end them? To lie, to tamper with the truth, yes
– and by tampering we seek to end
The heartaches and thousand shocks
That sincerity is heir to, 'tis a consummation
Devoutly to be wished. To lie, to be careless with the truth!
Ah, perchance to dream: ay, there's the rub;
For in that vale of despond dies vulgar verity
And when we have shuffled off this mortal coil
Must give us pause to respect that makes calamity of so long life;
For who would bear the whips and scorns accompanying
mawkish validity

The opposing ways, the proudman's half-truths
The pangs of despised love, the law's delay
The insolence of office and the spurning

That patient merit of the unworthy takes,
To coat the pill with simpering platitudes,
O truth thus maligned is dead as with the settlement of a
                                                    bare bodkin?
To live forever that lie, to grunt and sweat under a weary life
But that the dread of something after death,
The undiscovered country from whose bourn
No traveller returns, inhibits the will,
And makes us rather bear those truths known to us
Than fly to others that we know not of?
Thus conscience does make cowards of us all
And thus the nature has of resolution
Is sicklied over with the tendency to adapt,
To twist and torture – to stay stumb
And enterprise of great height and moment
With this regard their currents turn awry
And lose the name of action –

உ

Road to Joy

Grief has no place in poetry
Let it be banished
Exiled to the obituaries
Consigned to news bulletins

Let not sorrow stain the page
Nor spoil the symmetry of syntax
Relegate gloom to the gutter press
And other parasites of hate

Practice the quiet solitude of nuns
The joyous piety of monks
The lone pilgrim's excesses
That extinguish despair
In zealous fires of prophecies and visions

Subsume tragedy in Hellenic beauty
and noble crusades
Rapturous Eden before the serpent
Declare chivalry and requited love
With the trumpets of Zion

Write not of casualties nor refugees
Assume the discipline of minstrels
Who, forgetting discordant chords
Proclaim Beethoven's ninth extravagance

ఇ

My Cat

The sun raps at my door
I pick a handful of dandelions
For my cat

She is unimpressed,
Basking on a log pile
She ignores me for the sun

Midges cluster overhead
An angry bee drones away
Showered in grass clippings

Beyond the pond
The stream gurgles downhill
And is lost in the river

My cat yawns
Oblivious and indolent
Punished by sun and love

❧

You're Sacking Your Gardener

You're sacking your gardener
Who gathered the harvest of the heart
Who pruned your pride
To bring forth the buds of innocence
Who nurtured your borders and boundaries
Around your desperate yearning

You're dismissing your housekeeper
Who polished your desire
Who mopped up your lies
And hid your truth with facts
Who dusted around your sordid secrets
And sanitised your future

You're letting your cook go
Who catered to your whims
And served you with distinction
Who sated your cruel hunger
Who hosted your prim orgies
And gave away your just dessert

You're laying off your labourer
Who restored your sad refuge
Who built up your confidence
And demolished your defences
Slaving to hide your impatience
And bury your indifference

You're dispensing with your nurse
Who sat through long years of suffering
Breathing life into your negligence
To ease the nagging pain
And fought to save your credibility
With the blood-letting of humour

You chose the lonely option
The privilege of uncertainty
The route of cold rejection
Of neglected paths and grubby corridors
Of the heart with no companion
It was ever easy to do

❧

tabula rasa

the sky is heavy
light snow falling
tyres hum, my way is swift
snow sweeps my path
like wafts of foam
skudding over a windswept beach

looking back in the mirror
the fleeting flakes have gone
as my past merits no entry
in the Book of Sighs
'...never troubled the scorer!'
the pristine path mocks my passing

ॐ

Balanced Diet

I enjoy a balanced diet
I enjoy it every day
A kilo in the morning
A kilo come what may

I eat all within balance—
Pies before they're smutty
Then some beans on toast
Or perhaps a bacon-butty

Just a kilo I say
Sausages, eggs and chips
And in a balanced way
I've pounds upon my hips

Cheese and potato jacket
No need to stop and weigh
It's got it on the packet
In boldest-print display

Pizzas and fahitas
Add a spicy interlude
Or candy and cream cake
When I'm in the mood

Winegums to the left,
Jelly-babies to the right
Chochies, chochies, chochies
I'm counting them all night

The same is in one hand
As within the other
And if there's any over
I save them for my brother

It's just the simplest way
What's the point of scales?
And I know it's a good diet
For I've seen it in e-mails

And merely for the record
If there's anything I lack
I'm sure I'll make it up
In another healthy snack

Most of these daily diets
Are strictly for the birds
However, if I'm wrong
I'll gladly eat my words

☙

Questions

Will I again taste honey sips
Where two veiled rose petals meet
From loving warm and tender lips?

Shall I once more caress those hips
Shrouded close in a satin sheet
With cold trembling fingertips?

On days when raging tempest rips
Leaves from the trees along the street
And into dust our fever whips

May I yet dream of treasure ships
Or rainbows over fields of wheat
As into mine her hand she slips?

The clock tells me that dead time trips
On – never missing a beat
Despite those constant nagging blips

Is this the end of our eclipse?
Into dark eyes my being dips
As to the sun and me she skips

୧୬

You're leaving
The door has closed again
You're leaving
I can't remember when
I felt this way

I'm grieving
Gulls have flown inland
Deceiving
Dry pen in my hand
Nothing to say

The song-bird
Extracts a leaf
A wrong word
Reflects my grief
Forgive me now

In sorrow
I'll recall your name
Tomorrow
I shall write again
Maybe in the fall...

&

6 Bare Feet

One fat, one spotty and short
(the missing one was father)
Had come for an evening's sport
Upon Morecombe's Costa Brava

The middle one just wore a grin
As he surveyed the tide
His spectacles upon his chin
And feet upon his bride

'How brilliant to sit at rest,
All your day's work done;
Knitting your sister a cotton vest
And swallowing flies for fun!'

'I'm sure the sun is sinking,'
His friend said with a sneeze
'The sea it's started drinking
It must be on it's knees.'

They played a while upon the beach
On cornet and washing scrubber
Then floated off, just out of reach
On a mermaid made of rubber

And so the sun turned pink
Before their bloodshot eyes
It didn't so much sink
As gradually capsize

Now such is not an issue
In sunny Mogadishu
But caused quite a stir
On Morecombe's Riviere

∽

Mahogany

You gild me with a passion
That stirs the still pond to a frenzy
And spills sun on the silken flanks of dappled ponies

I long to gaze on your hair until I turn blind
Then comb it with burning fingers until it sings

I long to kiss your back until my lips bruise
And you are lost to slumber

I want to catch your breathing
And market it to the pure

I want to lay flowers at your feet
And fall asleep counting the petals

To dream only of you
And waken to you calling my name

Then trace your image across the sheets
Until I flow into it

I want to kneel at the altar of your body
Until I cannot stand

To be consumed within
Your tempestuous baptism of fire

Then lie in the sanctuary of your arms
Til I am born again

To learn that the beauty of your eyes and flesh
Are your soul's everyday clothes

Listen to the breeze
Carrying echoes of these whispers
Across the space between us

ℭℑ

And would I lie to you?

Never a thief nor liar be
We learnt that at our mother's knee
I lie, you lie, come lie with me
Let's lie beneath the greenwood tree
To lie and never count the cost
To lie when love's labour's lost
Come lie with me amid the heather
It's comforting to lie together
The lies we'd tell, we'd never lack
Between us we could tell a pack

My love was once so sweet to me
As the vine on yonder tree
Always there when I called
Our future lay in marble halls
She vowed an everlasting dream
But this was never as it seemed
'Ere she uttered a sultry sigh
Another chanced to catch her eye
We were left to live and let lie
As wondrous vows passed us by

Jackdaws bicker beyond my pane
In winter sunshine or summer rain
And from the pillow where I lie
I'll lie to you in a lullaby
From my casement I espy
Our rainbow falling from the sky
Forget the many lies I've told
Dappled hues don't end in gold

I lie, you lie, like victims in a dance
Caught in the rhythm of circumstance
You lie to me, I lie to you
Believing what others say is true
And would I lie to you?
When expedience is due
Perhaps the truth will lie
On the lips of a last goodbye

❧